D1710901

Heroes for Young Readers

Written by Renee Taft Meloche
Illustrated by Bryan Pollard

Adoniram Judson
Amy Carmichael
Bethany Hamilton
Betty Greene
Brother Andrew
Cameron Townsend
Corrie ten Boom
C. S. Lewis
David Livingstone
Eric Liddell
George Müller

Gladys Aylward
Hudson Taylor
Ida Scudder
Jim Elliot
Jonathan Goforth
Loren Cunningham
Lottie Moon
Mary Slessor
Nate Saint
Nick Vujicic
William Carey

Heroes of History for Young Readers

Written by Renee Taft Meloche
Illustrated by Bryan Pollard

Daniel Boone
Clara Barton
George Washington
George Washington Carver
Louis Zamperini
Meriwether Lewis

*Heroes for Young Readers Activity Guides and audio CDs
are also available. See the back of this book for more information.*

www.HeroesThenAndNow.com

HEROES OF HISTORY FOR YOUNG READERS

LOUIS ZAMPERINI

Survivor and Champion

Written by Renee Taft Meloche
Illustrated by Bryan Pollard

Emerald
Books

LYNNWOOD, WASHINGTON

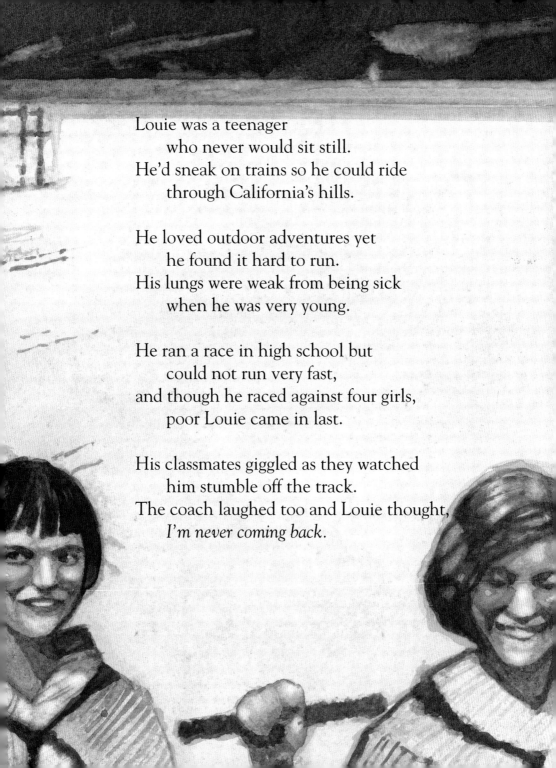

Louie was a teenager
  who never would sit still.
He'd sneak on trains so he could ride
  through California's hills.

He loved outdoor adventures yet
  he found it hard to run.
His lungs were weak from being sick
  when he was very young.

He ran a race in high school but
  could not run very fast,
and though he raced against four girls,
  poor Louie came in last.

His classmates giggled as they watched
  him stumble off the track.
The coach laughed too and Louie thought,
  I'm never coming back.

He hid beneath some bleachers and
      then walked home in defeat.
He told his older brother, "I'm
      not fast like you are, Pete."

So Pete made Louie run with him
      to help him to improve.
He'd whack him with a little stick
      to keep him on the move.

Soon Louie got much faster and
      improved in every race,
until one day he did so well
      he even won first place!

He trained so hard he soon became
    the very best by far:
the fastest high-school miler and
    his country's rising star.

When Louie turned nineteen he reached
    an even bigger dream.
He ran for the United States
    on their Olympic team.

He joined the army air force just
    as World War Two began.
He served in the Pacific in
    the battle with Japan.

He flew with other crewmen who
    were skilled and trained to fight.
One day they crossed the ocean when
    both engines quit in flight.

The plane began to slowly glide,
    then much to Louie's shock
it started shaking back and forth,
    then dropped down like a rock.

It hit the water, blew apart,
    but Louie had survived!
He saw a drifting raft he'd need
    to help him stay alive.

Though Louie's ribs were broken and
    he wore some heavy shoes,
he started swimming toward the raft.
    There was no time to lose.

He grabbed a long cord trailing from
    the raft and reeled it in,
then pulled the pilot Phil and crewman
    Mac on board with him.

He searched the raft and found some food,
    but it would not go far:
the three of them would have to share
    just six big chocolate bars.

He found fresh tins of water which
    was very happy news,
since water from the ocean was
    too poisonous to use.

The next day Louie went to get
    each man his chocolate treat,
yet as he looked he could not find
    a single bar to eat.

Mac's eyes were wide and full of guilt
    for he'd done something bad:
he'd eaten every chocolate bar,
    the only food they had.

It did not rain for six long days.
        Their water tins ran dry.
Unless the men had water soon,
        they knew that they would die.

That night as Louie listened while
        old hymns were sung by Phil,
he thought, *What if I prayed just like
        the time my mom got ill?*

He'd never read the Bible and
        did not like church one bit.
He knew God made the heavens and
        the earth but that was it.

Yet Louie bowed his head and meant
        each word he said in prayer:
"I promise if You'll make it rain,
        I'll serve You anywhere."

The sky soon opened up with rain.
        Then once the rain had stopped,
the grateful men drank from their tins,
        which they'd filled to the top.

When twenty-seven days had passed
   since they'd been lost at sea,
they saw a plane and waved their shirts.
   They screamed excitedly!

Then bullets started whizzing by
   and pouring down like rain.
It was the Japanese who came
   and flew the deadly plane.

As Louie watched in terror as
   some bullets hit their raft,
he dived into the water but
   a shark was coming fast!

The shark rushed straight for Louie's legs.
    He swung them to the side.
The shark then moved toward Louie's head,
    its jaws now open wide!

He smacked the shark right on its snout.
    It flinched, then swam from view.
He pulled himself back on the raft
    to join the other two.

Though forty-eight small bullet holes
    had pierced their living space,
the bullets had missed Phil and Mac,
    who thankfully were safe.

The raft was losing lots of air.
    They'd need their patching kit.
It sat low in the water and
    they'd need to fix it quick!

Then leaping from the water as
    it moved at lightning speed,
that same old shark was back again,
    determined to succeed.

The shark lunged straight at Louie and
    just what do you suppose?
Quick-thinking Louie grabbed an oar
    and bopped it on its nose.

Both Phil and Mac fought off more sharks
    while Louie made repairs.
He patched the tiny bullet holes
    and pumped the raft with air.

A shark surprised him from behind.
    Mac struck it with his oar.
This speedy act saved Louie's life,
    which he was grateful for.

The raft sat higher in the sea
    once all the holes were patched.
The hungry sharks gave up their search
    for someone they could snatch.

Days later in their yellow raft
        an empty space was there,
for Mac had gotten sick and died
        from lack of food and care.

Then on one stormy night the raft
        raced upward toward the sky
on giant waves that shot them up
        some forty-five feet high.

Although their raft remained afloat,
        they struggled to be brave,
as like a roller coaster they
        raced up and down each wave.

The storm raged on and tossed their raft
        throughout that fearful night,
but when the morning sun appeared,
        they saw green land in sight!

For forty-seven days they'd lived
    and suffered on the seas.
They now stepped on an island which
    was ruled by Japanese.

The Japanese placed both of them
    in dingy prison cells.
The cells had flies, mosquitoes, rats
    and icky, slimy smells.

The guards made Louie whistle, sing
    and dance around the place.
They jabbed him with sharp sticks and tossed
    hot tea right in his face.

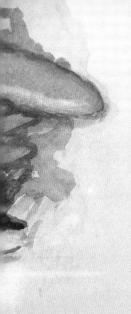

They shipped both Phil and Louie to
    a prison in Japan.
"Let's have some fun with Louie," said
    one guard. "I have a plan."

Since Louie had competed in
    the great Olympic Games,
the guards decided they would put
    this running star to shame.

Though Louie had no shoes to wear
    and had become quite thin,
they took their fastest runner and
    made Louie race with him.

To Louie's great surprise his legs
    felt light just like the breeze,
but Louie knew that if he won,
    the guards would not be pleased.

Yet Louie was too proud to lose
    and soon stepped up his pace.
He grabbed the lead and finished strong
    and won the two-man race!

As other prisoners watching him
    began to cheer and shout,
a guard got mad and swung his club
    and—*bam!*—knocked Louie out.

The worst guard there was called the Bird.
    He filled the men with dread.
One day he took his belt and cracked
    it hard on Louie's head.

The painful blow knocked Louie down
    and caused the room to spin.
As Louie's head began to bleed,
    the Bird began to grin.

So Louie tried to hide from him
    whenever he was near.
He prayed, "Please, God, help rescue me
    and get me out of here!"

He'd spent two years in prison when
    the war came to an end.
Both Phil and Louie were set free
    and sent back home again.

In Louie's dreams he saw the Bird.
    It made it hard to sleep.
For five long years the nightmares came,
    which often made him weep.

The Bird would rise up over him
    and whirl his belt and scream.
The belt would then come crashing down
    in Louie's scary dreams.

One night as Louie sat inside
    a giant circus tent,
he heard a preacher speak about
    God's love and what it meant.

He thought about the prayer he'd prayed
    so many years before,
that he would serve God if it rained
    and he survived the war.

He knew his promise on the raft
    was one he had not kept,
so when the service ended he
    got on his knees and wept.

He prayed, *I want to love You, God,*
    and keep my word to You.
I want to be both kind and good.
    Please show me what to do.

When Louie went to sleep that night,
    the Bird did not appear,
and from then on his nightmares stopped
    and he was free from fear.

Soon Louie started up a camp
      where boys could swim and bike.
He listened to their troubles as
      they went on mountain hikes.

He taught them how to climb down cliffs,
      in wintertime they skied,
and he became just like a dad
      to many kids in need.

At night around a campfire he
      would read the Bible too,
and tell them how his Christian faith
      gave him the peace he knew.

He served in churches, spoke in schools
      and even in the jails,
and many were inspired by
      his true, amazing tales.

In nineteen ninety-eight when he
    was almost eighty-one,
he carried the Olympic torch,
    still fit and strong to run.

These Winter Games brought memories
    of places he had known,
for he was in Japan again,
    where prison once was home.

Yet there was only love and joy
    that Louie felt that day
as crowds of Japanese all clapped
    and cheered him on his way.

He thought back on the war when he
    had often felt alone,
yet now he knew that he was never
    truly on his own.

Yes, God watched over Louie till
    the very day he died
at ninety-seven years of age,
    his Savior by his side.

Heroes for Young Readers and Heroes of History for Young Readers are based on the Christian Heroes: Then & Now and Heroes of History biographies by Janet & Geoff Benge. Don't miss out on these exciting, true adventures for ages 10 and up!

Christian Heroes: Then & Now

by Janet & Geoff Benge

Nate Saint: On a Wing and a Prayer
Paul Brand: Helping Hands
Rachel Saint: A Star in the Jungle
Rowland Bingham: Into Africa's Interior
Samuel Zwemer: The Burden of Arabia
Sundar Singh: Footprints Over the Mountains
Wilfred Grenfell: Fisher of Men
William Booth: Soup, Soap, and Salvation
William Carey: Obliged to Go

Heroes of History
by Janet & Geoff Benge

Abraham Lincoln: A New Birth of Freedom
Alan Shepard: Higher and Faster
Ben Carson: A Chance at Life
Benjamin Franklin: Live Wire
Billy Graham: America's Pastor
Captain John Smith: A Foothold in the New World
Christopher Columbus: Across the Ocean Sea
Clara Barton: Courage under Fire
Daniel Boone: Frontiersman
Davy Crockett: Ever Westward
Douglas MacArthur: What Greater Honor
George Washington: True Patriot
George Washington Carver: From Slave to Scientist
Harriet Tubman: Freedombound
John Adams: Independence Forever
Laura Ingalls Wilder: A Storybook Life
Meriwether Lewis: Off the Edge of the Map
Milton Hershey: More Than Chocolate
Orville Wright: The Flyer
Ronald Reagan: Destiny at His Side
Theodore Roosevelt: An American Original
Thomas Edison: Inspiration and Hard Work
William Penn: Liberty and Justice for All

Available in paperback, e-book, and audiobook formats.
Unit Study Curriculum Guides are available for each biography.